LEARN TO CROCHET
the Easy Way

by Jean Leinhauser

Produced by:
  The Creative Partners™ LLC

Photo Stylist:
  Carol Wilson Mansfield

Photography:
  James Jaeger

Book Design:
  Graphic Solutions, inc-chgo

A Note From Jean

You really, really want to learn to crochet.

But you don't know anyone who can teach you.

Can you learn, all by yourself, from a book?

Yes, you can! I taught myself from a book, and so have thousands of other crocheters.

And you can too! In just a few hours you too can learn the basics of crochet. Whether you are right handed or left handed, green thumbed or all thumbs, with just this book, a skein of yarn, a crochet hook and a pair of scissors, you can learn a new skill that will bring you pleasure for years to come.

Crochet is a favorite of international fashion designers, and on the runways garments with crochet trim, or even completely made in crochet, are regularly seen. Fashions aren't the only thing you can make with crochet. Crocheters love to make afghans, baby clothes, placemats, rugs, handbags, hats, scarves—the list of what you'll be able to make is endless.

Crochet is a versatile medium: it can be worked flat in rows, as a tube, in circles or squares, or even in curlicues. It can be used to make a smooth surface, or bumps, or loops or puffs. It can be worked as a dense fabric or as delicate open lace. There is no end to what you can do with crochet. This book will show you all of the basic stitches and techniques, and as you learn them you will actually work a swatch to help your fingers learn what to do.

When you visit a store to buy your supplies, you'll be fascinated by all the wonderful yarns that are available today in a wide variety of textures and colors.

To start the lessons, set aside at least two hours that you can devote to learning this wonderful new skill. Then come along with me and let's start the crochet adventure!

And-once you've learned to crochet, you may want to try one of the patterns I have included which have been written especially for beginners.

Jean Leinhauser

Jean Leinhauser

CONTENTS

GETTING STARTED

WHAT TO BUY...

You are going to need just a few things to get started: a crochet hook, a ball or skein of yarn, a pair of scissors – and most important, a two-hour time block when you can work quietly with interruptions only for emergencies!

Later you will learn all you need to know about yarns and hooks, but right now you just need to buy:

- A skein or ball of a type of yarn called "worsted weight" in a light or medium color. No dark colors please! You want to be able to see every stitch clearly.

- A crochet hook, aluminum or plastic, in a size marked "H" or 5 mm.

- A large plastic sewing needle with a big eye, usually called a yarn needle.

You'll also want to have on hand a pair of sharp scissors.

SETTING THE STAGE FOR LEARNING...

You've planned to set aside two hours to devote to learning the basics. Now choose a comfortable place to work, with good lighting. To make it easier to switch from watching your hands to referring to the diagrams in this book, you may want to sit at a table.

Turn off the television and the music; put the telephone answering machine on, and turn off the cell phone; put the cat and the new puppy in another room; tell the kids you can be interrupted only in case of their bodily injury, and ignore the doorbell.

Now let's crochet!

ABOUT YOUR YARN...

Your yarn is probably packaged in a skein (pronounced "skane") or ball. It may be what is called a "pull skein," meaning that you can pull the yarn from the center as you work.

Read the yarn label, and if it is a pull skein, the label will tell you first to pull out a yarn end from one side, then work with the yarn end at the opposite side. If the label does not mention this, it is probably not a pull skein, and you will need to remove the paper label and use the yarn from the outside of the skein.

Tip: To keep the yarn skein from rolling all over, keep a clean wastebasket by your side and put the yarn in it.

PART ONE: LEARNING THE BASICS

Lesson 1: Hooks and Yarn

GETTING TO KNOW THE HOOK

Crochet hooks are engineered to make your work easier and more uniform and have areas that you need to know. These areas are indicated in **Fig 1**.

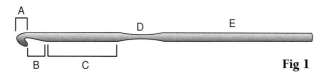

Fig 1

(A) Head: this is the "business end" of the hook, which will slide in and out of the work as needed, and which will grab or hook the yarn so you can draw it through easily. Different brands have heads that are shaped differently, but they all are used in the same way.

(B) Throat: This is the slanted part from the head to the working area. Never work on the throat, or your stitches will be much too tight.

(C) Working area: This is the most important part of the hook. Here, on this straight area, the stitches are formed and "set" into their final size. Be sure all stitches are worked well up on this area.

(D) Finger hold: Many hooks have an indented space where you can place your thumb to help balance the work. Other hooks eliminate the finger hold. Which type you prefer is up to you; they both work equally well. Stitches should never be formed on the finger hold, or they will be much too loose.

(E) Shaft: This is the part of the hook on which you will rest your hand as you work.

Crochet hooks come in a variety of sizes (see page 29). These sizes are usually marked right on the hook as either a letter or number and usually also in millimeters. They are made in a variety of materials, such as aluminum, steel, plastic or wood. For our lessons, you will use a Size H (5mm) hook in aluminum or plastic.

HOLDING THE HOOK

Most crocheters hold the hook in the dominant hand in one of two ways: the knife hold or the pencil hold.

The Knife Hold: Hold the hook as you hold a knife to cut your dinner (**Fig 2**).

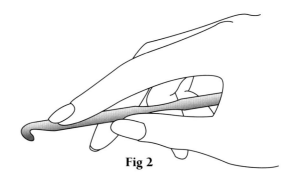

Fig 2

The Pencil Hold: Hold the hook as you would a pen or pencil (**Fig 3**).

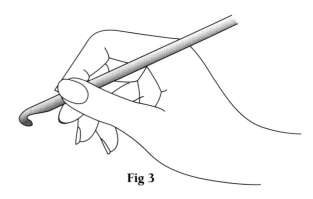

Fig 3

Use whichever method you find more comfortable; there is no right or wrong way to hold the hook.

HOLDNG THE YARN

The yarn, too, should be held the way that is most comfortable for you. Hold the yarn in the non-dominant hand. Some people like to weave the yarn through their fingers (**Fig 4**), others just pick it up and hold it lightly against their palm with their ring and little fingers.

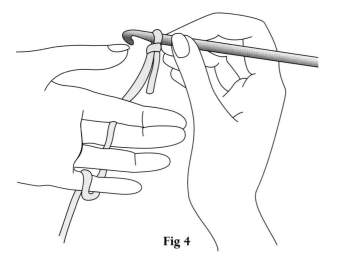

Fig 4

The thumb, index and middle fingers do most of the work. Again, there are two ways to hold the working yarn, and whichever is most natural for you is the one you should use.

Index Finger Hold: Here the index finger and thumb hold the yarn against the hook (**Fig 5**) and the middle finger directs the yarn and controls the tension.

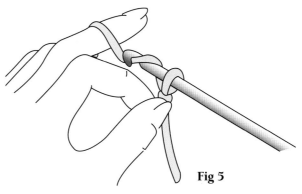

Fig 5

Middle Finger Hold: The middle finger and thumb hold the yarn against the hook and the index finger directs the yarn from the skein or ball and controls the tension.

Try holding the yarn both ways, and choose which way is best for you.

Tip: *No matter what any so-called "expert" tells you, there is no wrong way to hold the hook or the yarn. The right way is the way that works for you and gives you the results you want.*

Lesson 2: The Slip Knot and The Chain Stitch

THE SLIP KNOT

All crochet begins with making a slip knot (sometimes called a slip loop) on the hook. To do this, place the end of the yarn on a flat surface and, leaving a 6" end, make a loop as shown in **Fig 6**. Insert the hook as shown in **Fig 6** and draw the loop up onto the hook by pulling on the end marked A. The knot should be snug on the hook, but not tight, and should slide easily. Be sure to leave the loose yarn end at least 6" long to use later (**Fig 7**).

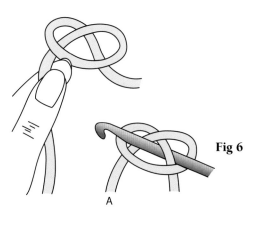

Fig 6

A

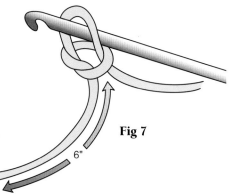

6"

Fig 7

Tip: The slip knot is never counted as a stitch. It is used only to start a new piece or section of crochet or to join new yarn. Patterns rarely tell you to make the slip knot; it is assumed that you know to do this whenever you start a new piece of crochet.

THE CHAIN

The word "chain" can be confusing in crochet, as it is used to mean a single stitch and also a group of stitches. The chain is the foundation on which all crochet is built. It is rather like the bottom row of bricks in a brick wall: without that bottom row, there would be no brick wall.

To practice the chain, first make a slip knot on the hook. Hold the hook in your dominant hand and the yarn in the other hand. Take the yarn from back to front over the hook and catch it with the hook head (**Fig 8**) and draw it through the slip knot on the hook and up onto the working area of the hook: you have now made one chain stitch.

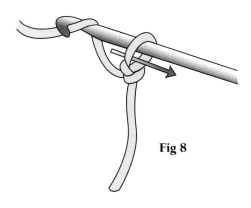

Fig 8

*Tip: In crochet, always take the yarn over the hook from back to front, never from front to back (**Fig 9**).*

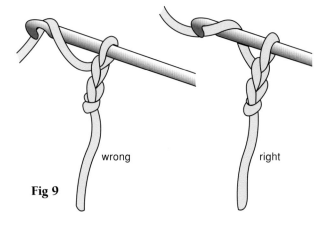

wrong   right

Fig 9

8

Once again, take the yarn from back to front over the hook, catch it and draw it through the loop on the hook (which is the first chain you made). You have now made two chain stitches. Make these chain stitches loosely, because you will be working into them later.

Don't worry about working too loosely – your chains will become the correct size as you become more experienced. Be sure to work each stitch only on the working area of the hook (**Fig 10**).

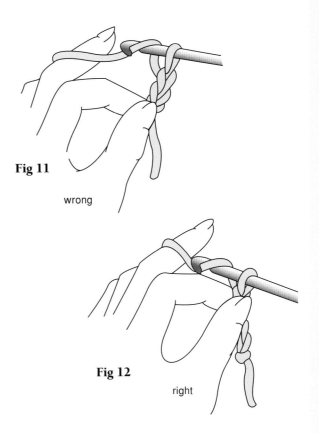

Fig 11

wrong

Fig 12

right

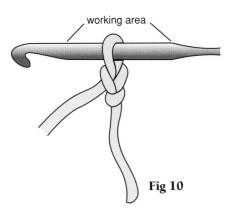

working area

Fig 10

Continue making additional chain stitches in this manner; as you work and the group of chain stitches grows longer, keep moving your fingers up closer to the hook after each stitch or two to help maintain control. **Figs 11 and 12** show the right and wrong placement for your fingers. Continue making chains, taking care to take the yarn from back to front for each stitch, and to form stitches on the working area of the hook. The group of chain stitches you are making is called the "starting chain" or the "beginning chain"; these terms always refer to a group of chain stitches.

By now you've been concentrating and working hard, and it's time to take a break! First, take your hook out of the work; now pull on the yarn and rip out all the chain stitches you have made! Don't panic! You'll start again with the next lesson and make them even better.

Get up, walk around, get a cup of tea or coffee and relax for a few minutes.

THE LANGUAGE OF CROCHET

Crochet instructions are written with many abbreviations; this helps to keep the printed instructions of a manageable length. Although this may be confusing at first, you'll soon learn to recognize these abbreviations. Pages 26 and 27 have a list of standard abbreviations and symbols used in most crochet patterns. The following stitch instructions give you the name of the stitch written out (as in "single crochet") and then tell you how it is abbreviated (as in "sc"). From then on, we will usually use the abbreviation so that you will get accustomed to using it.

Lesson 3: The Single Crochet Stitch

Abbreviation: **sc**

Now it's time to get back to work, and to learn another stitch. Most crochet is worked with variations of four different stitches: single crochet (the shortest), half double crochet, double crochet and triple crochet (the tallest). The difference is in their height. To work any of these stitches, you'll need to make a starting chain, and then work the stitches into it.

WORKING INTO THE CHAIN

Following the steps in the last lesson, make a slip knot on the hook and make 21 chain stitches. In counting stitches in crochet, never count the slip knot, or the stitch on the hook. **Fig 13** shows how to count.

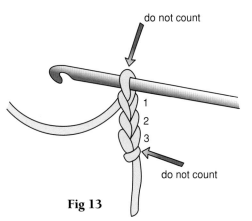

Fig 13

Now look at the completed chain (**Fig 14**): the front will look like a series of interlocked Vs, and each V represents one chain stitch. Flip the chain

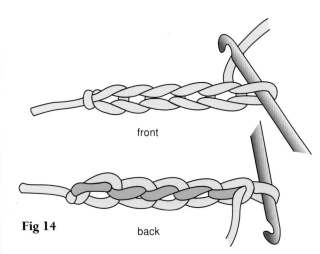

Fig 14

over and look at the back, where you will see a row of bumps. Each bump also represents one chain stitch: each V has a corresponding bump.

When working the first row of stitches into a starting chain, you will always need to skip one or more stitches first, depending on how tall the new stitch will be. You can never work into the very first chain from the hook, as it will unravel.

For sc (remember, that is the abbreviation for single crochet), you will skip one chain stitch.

FIRST SINGLE CROCHET ROW (Right Side)

Step 1: Hold the chain of 21 chain stitches with the V side facing you, and the row of chains to your left. Skip the first chain stitch from the hook and insert the hook from top to bottom in the back bump (**Fig 15**) of the next chain stitch.

Fig 15

Step 2: Hook the yarn and draw it through to the front and up onto the working area of the hook. (**Fig 16**): there are now 2 loops on the hook (**Fig 17**).

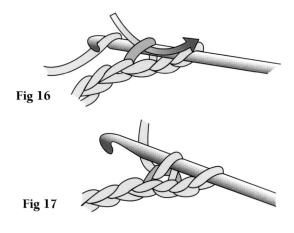

Fig 16

Fig 17

Step 3: Take the yarn over the hook again from back to front (this is called "yarn over"), hook it and draw it through both loops on the hook: one loop now remains on the hook and you have completed one sc stitch.

Tip: As you draw the loop through, roll the hook slightly toward you with the head pointing slightly downward; this makes it easier to pull the loop through.

Now insert the hook from top to bottom in the back bump of the next chain stitch and repeat Steps 2 and 3: You have made another sc stitch.

Continue to work in this manner across the entire chain; your work will look like **Fig 18**. Work into the last chain stitch, but not into the slip knot. At the end of the row, you will have made 20 sc stitches, and one loop will remain on the hook.

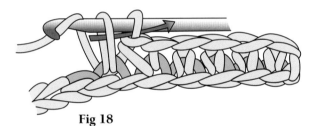

Fig 18

Tip: The loop on the hook is never counted as a stitch.

Tip: Never work into the slip knot.

To work another row of sc stitches, you will need to turn the piece and work back into the sc stitches you just made. Whenever you turn the work to start a new row, you will need to first work one or more chain stitches to bring the yarn up to the height of the next row. This is called the turning chain. For sc, you will need

to work only one chain. So make one chain and turn the work counter clockwise (**Fig 19**).

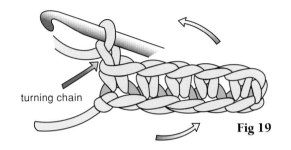

turning chain

Fig 19

Tip: Always leave the hook in the work as you turn.

Tip: As you work, you may find that the yarn sometimes splits. This is not your fault! Yarn is made up of a number of strands, or plies, that are twisted together, and they sometimes untwist as you are working. In this case, pull out a stitch or two until you reach where the yarn split, then remake the stitches.

SECOND SINGLE CROCHET ROW (Wrong Side)

You will never work into a turning chain unless a pattern specifically tells you to do so.

So in this case, skip the turning chain and work one sc in the sc nearest to your hook (**Fig 20**). (This is actually the last sc worked on the first row.)

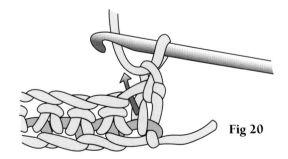

Fig 20

Since you are now working into a stitch, not a chain, insert the hook under the top two loops of the stitch, and repeat Steps 2 and 3 of the first row. Work one sc in each stitch across the row. You should still have 20 single crochet stitches.

*Note: Count your stitches carefully; if you have more than 20 stitches, you may have worked a stitch into the turning chain at the right edge of the piece, or you may have worked two stitches into one stitch. If you have fewer than 20 stitches, you may have skipped a stitch or failed to work into the very last stitch (**Fig 21**). If necessary, remove the hook from the loop and rip out the row, then rework it carefully, counting the stitches.*

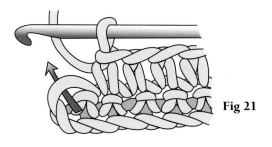

Fig 21

Tip: Even experienced crocheters do a lot of ripping out and reworking; in fact crocheters laughingly call ripping out "frogging" (rippit, rippit, rippit). So don't be concerned if you find yourself ripping frequently.

Now is a good time to take another break. Whenever you want to stop temporarily in your work, be sure to stop at the end of a row. Draw the loop on the hook up about a half inch (to keep the work from unraveling) and remove the hook. Put the hook down in a safe place where toddlers and kittens can't find it. You've probably been holding your work tightly, so flex your fingers and relax a bit.

When your break is over, work one more row of sc stitches, remembering to ch 1 and turn at the end of each row. Work as many rows of single crochet as you need to feel comfortable with the stitch. With each additional row you work, your stitches will become more even and more attractive.

HOW TO SHAPE CROCHET

When making a crochet project, you will often need to shape the piece. This is done by increasing (making the piece wider) and decreasing (making the piece narrower).

Unless otherwise specified, increasing is done by working 2 stitches in one stitch. Decreasing is more complicated, as there is a different method used for each stitch.

DECREASING IN SINGLE CROCHET

There are two ways to do this. When a pattern tells you to decrease in sc, you may use whichever decrease you prefer.

Method 1: Continuing on your sample swatch, ch 1 and turn. Sc in the first 2 stitches; now skip the next stitch (do not work into it), and sc in the next 4 stitches: you have decreased one stitch by skipping a stitch. Again skip one stitch, and sc in the next 4 stitches: you have decreased another stitch. This method of decreasing leaves a slight hole in the work.

Method 2: Insert the hook into the next stitch and draw up a loop; insert the hook in the next stitch and again draw up a loop: you now have 3 loops on the hook; yarn over and draw it through all 3 loops on the hook: you have now decreased one stitch; sc in the next 4 stitches, then draw up a loop in each of the next 2 stitches, yarn over and draw through all 3 loops on the hook: another stitch is decreased.

You now have 16 stitches; ch 1, turn. Work one more row of single crochet on these 16 stitches, ch 1, turn.

Now look at the work and see the difference in the appearance of the two decreases: there is a small hole where Method 1 was used, and a small bump where Method 2 was used.

INCREASING IN SINGLE CROCHET

Single crochet in each of the first 3 stitches, then work 2 single crochet stitches in the next st: you have increased one stitch. Continue practicing increases (work 2 stitches in one stitch) across the row. At the end of the row, do not work a turning chain. Instead, cut the yarn, leaving a 6" yarn end. With your hook draw this end through the last loop on the hook (**Fig 22**). This fastens the end so it won't pull out. Leave the end loose for now; later on you will weave it in securely. This way of ending the work may be called "finish off," "end off," or "fasten off" in instructions. They all mean the same thing.

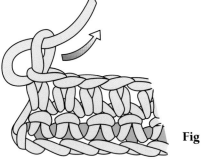

Fig 22

Tip: *Save this sample of single crochet for reference. You might want to attach a tag and identify it as single crochet. You will be making several swatches of different stitches and techniques which you can keep in a notebook.*

Lesson 4: The Half Double Crochet Stitch

Abbreviation: **hdc**

Hdc is a taller stitch than sc. For the sample swatch, make a slip knot on the hook and chain 21 sts.

FIRST HALF DOUBLE CROCHET ROW (Right Side)

Step 1: Yarn over the hook; insert the hook into the back bump of the 3rd ch from the hook; yarn over and draw up a loop: 3 loops are now on the hook.

Step 2: Yarn over again and draw the yarn though all 3 loops on the hook at one time (**Fig 23**): one hdc stitch is completed.

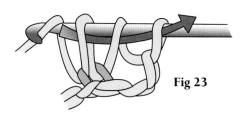

Fig 23

Repeat Steps 1 and 2 in each chain across the row, but in Step 1 insert the hook in the next chain instead of in the 3rd chain from the hook. At the end of the row you will have 20 hdc stitches, counting the first 2 chains you skipped at the beginning of the row as one stitch. Work the last stitch into the top ch; ch 1 and turn the work counter-clockwise.

SECOND HALF DOUBLE CROCHET ROW (Wrong Side)

Repeat Steps 1 and 2, working in stitches not chains, in each stitch across, ch 1 and turn. Work as many rows as you need to feel comfortable with the stitch. At the end of the last row, ch 1 and turn.

DECREASING IN HALF DOUBLE CROCHET

Hdc in each of the next 2 stitches; then decrease as follows:

Step 1: Yarn over, insert the nook in the next stitch and draw up a loop: 3 loops now on hook.

Step 2: Yarn over, insert the hook in the next stitch and draw up a loop: 5 loops now on hook.

Step 3: Yarn over and draw through all 5 loops on hook: hdc decrease made.

Tip: *To make drawing the yarn through 5 loops easier, hold the 5 loops firmly together with the fingers of the left hand.*

Hdc in the next 3 stitches, then work another hdc decrease; continue in this manner across the row; ch 1 and turn.

INCREASING IN HALF DOUBLE CROCHET

Hdc in the next 2 stitches, work 2 hdc in the next stitch: an increase made; continue practicing hdc increases across the row. At the end of the row, do not chain or turn; finish off and mark the sample as hdc.

Note: *In some patterns, a ch 2 rather than a ch 1, is used to turn hdc rows. If so, the ch 2 is usually counted as the first stitch of the following row. The pattern will usually tell you if this is done.*

Lesson 5: The Double Crochet Stitch

Abbreviation: **dc**

Dc stitches are taller than sc and hdc stitches. Crochet stitches are made taller by adding "yarn overs". To practice double crochet, first make slip knot and then make 22 chain stitches.

FIRST DOUBLE CROCHET ROW (Right Side)

Step 1: Bring the yarn over the hook from back to front, then insert the hook into the back bump of the fourth chain from the hook (**Fig 24**).

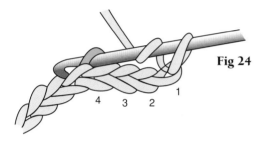

Fig 24

Step 2: Hook the yarn and draw it through the fourth chain and up onto the working area of the hook: the loop should be about ¾" tall: there are now 3 loops on the hook (**Fig 25**).

Fig 25

Step 3: Hook the yarn again, and draw it through the first two loops on the hook (**Fig 26**): 2 loops are now on the hook.

Fig 26

Step 4: Hook the yarn again and draw it through the remaining 2 loops (**Fig 27**): You have now made one dc stitch.

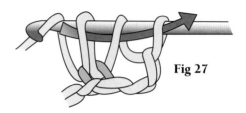

Fig 27

To work the next dc stitch, repeat Step 1, but insert the hook into the back bump of the next chain, rather than the fourth chain from the hook. Then repeat Steps 2 through 4 again. Continue in this manner, always working Step 1 into the next chain, across the whole starting chain. Count your stitches: counting those first 3 skipped chains as a stitch, you should now have 20 dc stitches. If your count is different, you may have forgotten to work into the very last stitch, or you may have accidentally worked 2 dc stitches into one of the chains. If the count is incorrect, pull out the work and start again.

To work the next row, you will again need to work a turning chain, and turn the work.

Because the dc stitches are taller than sc and hdc stitches, this time you will need to make 3 chains, to bring the yarn up to the correct height, then turn the work counter-clockwise as before (**Fig 28**).

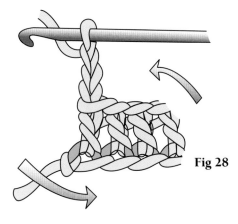

Fig 28

SECOND DOUBLE CROCHET ROW (Wrong Side)

The turning chain of 3 chain stitches counts as the first dc of this new row. Because of this, you will work your next dc in the 2nd stitch of the previous row, rather than the first stitch. **Fig 29** shows the wrong and the right placement for this stitch. It is very important to place this stitch correctly. Remember that the turning chain always counts as the first dc of the row, unless a pattern tells you otherwise.

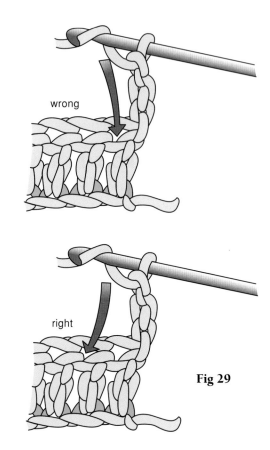

wrong

right

Fig 29

Now you will be working dc stitches into the stitches of the previous row.

*Tip: Knowing where to insert your hook is sometimes confusing; you must find the top of a given stitch. The V formed by the 2 loops just to the right of a stitch is the top (**Fig 30**) when working a right-side row, and to the left when working a wrong-side row.*

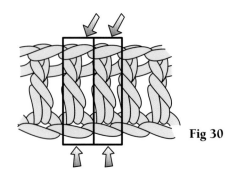

Fig 30

16

This is true for sc, hdc, dc and all other stitches.

Step 1: Yarn over, insert hook under the top 2 loops (the V) of the next stitch and draw up a loop the same height as the 3 turning chains: you now have 3 loops on the hook.

Step 2: Yarn over and draw it through the first 2 loops on the hook: 2 loops remain on the hook.

Step 3: Yarn over and draw it through the remaining 2 loops: you have completed one dc stitch.

Continue to work dc stitches in each stitch across the row. At the end, work the last dc into the top chain of the turning chain of the previous row (**Fig 31**). Be careful not to miss this last stitch. Counting the turning chain at the right-hand edge of the row as a stitch, you now have 20 dc stitches.

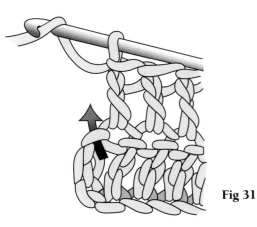

Fig 31

Work the turning chain as before, and continue to work in double crochet rows until you feel comfortable with the stitch. Now it's time to learn how to work decreases and increases in dc.

DECREASING IN DOUBLE CROCHET

Continuing on your practice piece, ch 3 and turn; work 3 dc stitches, then work a decrease as follows:

Step 1: Yarn over, insert the hook in the next stitch and draw up a loop, yarn over again and draw through the first 2 loops on the hook: 2 loops remain on the hook.

Step 2: Yarn over and insert the hook in the next stitch and draw up a loop: there are now 4 loops on the hook.

Step 3: Yarn over again and draw through the first 2 loops on the hook: 3 loops remain on the hook.

Step 4: Yarn over and draw through the remaining 3 loops: you have now worked a dc decrease.

Work 3 more dc stitches, then practice a dc decrease again. Work 3 more dc stitches, then another decrease; dc in the last 4 stitches; chain 3 and turn.

INCREASING IN DOUBLE CROCHET

Dc in the first 3 stitches. To add one stitch, work 2 dc stitches in the next stitch; dc in the next 3 stitches, then work an increase again. Practice increases across. At the end of the row, do not work the turning chain. Instead cut the yarn, leaving a 6" end, and finish off as you did for the previous samples. Mark this sample as dc.

Lesson 6: The Triple Crochet Stitch

Abbreviation: **tr** or **trc**

Triple crochet is sometimes called treble crochet in instructions. It is a tall stitch that works up quickly. For practice, make 23 chains.

FIRST TRIPLE CROCHET ROW (Right Side)

Step 1: Yarn over the hook twice, then insert the hook in the back bump of the 5th chain from the hook (**Fig 32**).

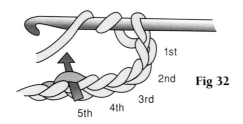

Fig 32

Step 2: Yarn over and draw through the chain and up to about 1" high: there are now 4 loops on the hook (**Fig 33**).

Fig 33

Step 3: Yarn over again and draw through the first 2 loops on the hook: there are now 3 loops on the hook.

Step 4: Yarn over and draw through the first 2 loops on the hook: 2 loops remain on the hook.

Step 5: Yarn over and draw through the remaining 2 loops. You have now completed one tr stitch (**Fig 34**).

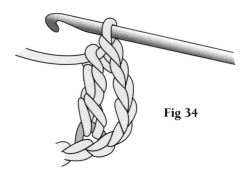

Fig 34

Repeat Steps 1 through 5 in the back bump of each chain across the row, working Step 1 in the next chain rather than the 4th chain from the hook. At the end, there will be 20 tr stitches, counting the first 4 skipped chains as a stitch; chain 4 and turn.

SECOND TRIPLE CROCHET ROW (Wrong Side)

Just as in double crochet, the turning chain counts as the first stitch of this new row.

So remember to skip the first stitch, and place the next triple crochet in the 2nd stitch.

Repeat Steps 1 through 5 in each stitch across; ch 5 and turn for the next row.

Work as many more rows as you need to feel comfortable with the tr stitch; now practice decreasing in tr.

DECREASING IN TRIPLE CROCHET

At end of the last row, ch 4 and turn; remember that the ch 4 counts as the first stitch of the new row; tr in the next 2 stitches. Work a decrease as follows:

Step 1: Yarn over twice, insert hook in the next stitch and draw up a 1" high loop; yarn over and draw through the first 2 loops on the hook; yarn over again and draw through the first 2 loops: 2 loops remain on the hook.

Step 2: Yarn over twice, insert hook in next stitch and draw up a 1" loop; yarn over and draw through the first 2 loops; yarn over again and draw through the first 2 loops: 3 loops remain.

Step 3: Yarn over and draw through the remaining 3 loops: you have now completed one tr decrease.

Tr in the next 2 stitches, then work another decrease; continue in this manner across the row; ch 4 and turn.

INCREASING IN TRIPLE CROCHET

Tr in the next 2 stitches, then work 2 tr stitches in the next stitch: you have increased one stitch; tr in the next 2 stitches, work an increase again; work in same manner across the row.

At the end of the row, do not chain or turn the work; finish off and mark the swatch as triple crochet.

Lesson 7: The Slip Stitch

Abbreviation: **sl st**

Sl st is a versatile stitch that is used to move yarn across a row without adding height, and to join stitches or new yarn.

JOINING NEW YARN

Take any one of your swatches, and hold it with the right side facing you, and the last row at the top. Make a slip knot on the hook, leaving a 6" yarn end, then insert the hook in the first stitch at your right; yarn over the hook and draw it completely through the stitch and through the slip knot: you have now joined a new piece of yarn with a sl st.

MOVING WITHOUT HEIGHT

Insert the hook in the next stitch, yarn over and draw it through the stitch and through the loop on the hook: another sl st made. Do this 3 more times. Now insert the hook in the next stitch and chain 3: this chain counts as a dc; work dc sts in each remaining stitch across the row. Look at your work and you will see that you have moved across a few stitches without adding height, then started working dc stitches. This method is often used in shaping necklines or underarms of garments. Finish off the piece.

Another way to use the sl st will be covered on page 23.

What You Have Learned...

You have now learned the six basic stitches of crochet: the chain, single crochet, half double crochet, double crochet, triple crochet and slip stitch. There are stitches that are even taller than triple crochet, which are made by adding additional yarn overs at the beginning of the stitch, but they are not used very often. When they are, the pattern you are using will give you specific instructions for these stitches.

The photo shows you how stitches vary in height. It shows 4 rows worked in sc, then in hdc, dc and tr. Note that although the stitches grow taller, they are all the same width.

4 rows
Triple Crochet

4 rows
Double Crochet

4 rows
Half Double
Crochet

4 rows
Single Crochet

Tip: Unless otherwise specified in instructions, remember these:

Turning Chains:

1 turning chain for sc; it does not count as a stitch

1 turning chain for hdc; it does not count as a stitch

3 turning chains for dc: they do count as a stitch

4 turning chains for tr: they do count as a stitch

Tip: Some publishers put the instructions for the turning chain at the end of a row, others place it at the beginning of the next row. The result is the same.

WORKING INTO THE STARTING CHAIN

For sc, work in the 2nd ch from the hook; the skipped chains do not count as a stitch; you need to make one more chain than the final number of stitches you need.

For hdc, work in the 3rd ch from the hook; the skipped chains do count as a stitch; you need to make 2 more chains than the final number of stitches you need.

For dc, work in the 4th ch from the hook; the skipped chains do count as a stitch; you need to make two more chains than the final number of stitches you need.

For tr, work in the 5th ch from the hook; the skipped chains do count as a stitch; you need to make 3 more chains than the final number of stitches you need.

PART TWO: THE IMPORTANCE OF GAUGE

If you want the garments you make to fit correctly; if you want the afghans you make to be the right size; and if you want to be sure you have enough yarn to finish a project, then you need to follow the gauge given in a pattern.

Gauge is the number of stitches and rows per inch that you get when you work with a specified yarn with a specified hook. Gauge is usually written like this:

Gauge
7 dc = 3 1/2"
6 dc rows = 4"

Before starting a project, it is important for you to make a sample swatch, using the same yarn specified in the pattern, and the same size hook. If just one hook size is specified in the pattern materials, make the swatch with that size hook. If two or more hook sizes are specified, the pattern should tell you which size to use for the gauge.

For the gauge listed above, you will need to work a swatch that will have 7 dc in the center, plus at least 3 extra dc on each side; so you will need 13 dc. Referring to the information on page 21, you see that you will need 3 extra chains to work in dc, so ch 16, then dc in the fourth chain from the hook and in each remaining chain. That will give you the 13 needed dc stitches.

Now look at the row gauge: 6 dc rows = 4"; so work 6 dc rows, plus two extra rows before and after, or a total of 10 rows. You need the extra stitches and rows because you are going to measure the gauge in the center of the swatch.

When the swatch is completed place it on a flat surface without stretching the piece.

Use a ruler to measure the stitches and rows in the center. If you have more stitches and rows per inch than specified, you are going to need to work the pattern with a larger hook. If you don't have as many as specified, then you need to use a smaller hook.

Don't just change to a different hook: you need to start again with a smaller or larger hook and work another swatch. You're anxious to get started on your project, and chances are you really don't want to take the time to make a gauge swatch. But do it anyway! Better to take a few minutes now than to be disappointed when the entire project is finished.

Many crochet patterns will give you only a stitch gauge, and not a row gauge. If so, then the row gauge is not important to the appearance of the pattern. But if the pattern gives both the sitch and the row gauge, then you need to get both.

Tip: *When both are given, first get the stitch gauge. It is then easy to adjust the row gauge.*

TO ADJUST THE ROW GAUGE

Work a dc as follows: yarn over the hook, insert hook in the next stitch and draw up a loop—then stop. This loop is the key to the height of the stitch; if your row gauge is not tall enough, draw this loop up a bit higher; if it is too tall, draw it up shorter. Then complete the dc in the usual manner. This works for any stitch; you can adjust the height of that first loop for sc, hdc, tr, or any other stitch.

PART THREE: THINGS YOU NEED TO KNOW

Finishing

When a crochet piece has been completed, you need to do some finishing.

WEAVING IN ENDS

On the practice swatches you have been making, you've left the yarn ends at the beginning and end of the swatch just hanging there loosely. On an actual project, these ends would be neatly woven in so that they do not pull loose. To practice this, take one of your swatches and thread one of the ends into the large-eyed yarn needle. Working on the wrong side of the swatch, weave the needle in and out of the backs of several stitches, then weave again in another direction. Do this until the 6" of yarn is used up. Then pull out the yarn needle and clip the yarn off evenly. Do this with all the ends on your swatches.

JOINING CROCHET PIECES

If you are making a project with several pieces, you will need to join them in some manner. Sewing them leaves a fairly flat seam, and is easy to do. Hold two pieces with their right sides together, so that you are stitching on the wrong side. Thread an 18" yarn length into the yarn needle, and anchor the yarn by running it through the backs of stitches for a few inches. Then bring the needle from the back through the top two loops of the first stitch of the bottom piece, then through the top two loops of the front piece; pull the yarn all the way through, making the stitch snug but not tight. Take the yarn over the work and to the back again, then again bring the needle through the top two loops of both stitches, draw the yarn up snugly, then take it over the work

and to the back again. This is called the overcast stitch (**Fig 35**).

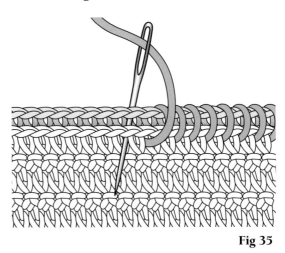

Fig 35

Instead of sewing, you can join in the same manner by working sc to join corresponding stitches, but this gives a bulkier seam.

GOING IN CIRCLES

All your practice so far has been working in rows. Crochet can also be worked in circles, squares, or other shapes.

To do this, instructions will tell you to work a certain number of chs, then join them with a slip stitch to form a ring (**Fig 36**). Then you will chain a certain number of stitches and either work into the ring (**Fig 37**), or into the next stitch.

Fig 36

Fig 37

FRONT LOOP, BACK LOOP

You have been working under both loops of each stitch. Some patterns will tell you to work only in the front loop, or only in the back loop. The front loop is the loop toward you; the back loop is the loop away from you (**Fig 38**).

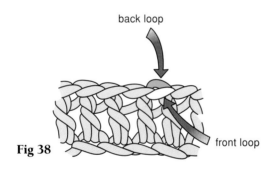

back loop

Fig 38   front loop

RIGHT SIDE, WRONG SIDE

The right side of a crochet piece is the side that will be worn on the outside, if the project is a garment; or the side that will usually be up if it is something like an afghan or a placemat.

When the pattern says "with right side facing" or "with wrong side facing" it means to hold the work with the right (or wrong) side facing you.

RIGHT SLEEVE, LEFT SLEEVE

In a pattern for a garment, right and left refer to the actual body part on which the garment part will be worn: the right or left arm, the right or left shoulder, etc.

RIGHT-HAND CORNER, LEFT-HAND CORNER

You may be told to join yarn, or do some other action, in the right-hand or left-hand corner. This means the corner closest to your right (or left) hand.

POST STITCHES

These are stitches that are worked around the vertical bar (called the post) of a stitch They are usually worked in double crochet, but can be worked in other stitches.

To work a double crochet front post stitch, yarn over the hook, then insert the hook from the front to the back to the front again around the post of the specified stitch (**Fig 39**), then complete the dc as usual. The front post stitch is usually worked on the right side of the piece.

To work a double crochet back post stitch, yarn over the hook, then insert the hook from the back to the front to the back again around the post of the specified stitch (**Fig 40**), then complete the dc as usual. The back post stitch is usually worked on the wrong side of the piece.

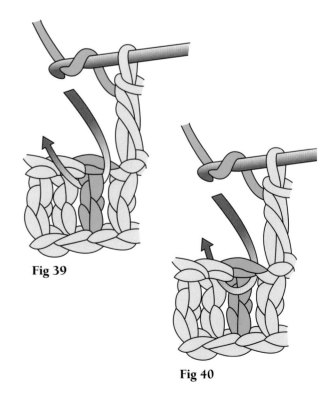

Fig 39

Fig 40

REVERSE SINGLE CROCHET

This is a stitch that gives a nice corded edging, but is sometimes confusing to learn as it is worked from left to right for right-handers, and right to left for left handers.

To work the stitch, first make one chain, then in the next st (**Fig 41**) work a single crochet in the usual manner; you'll have to wiggle the hook around a bit to make it go into the stitch to the right (or left), but it does work! Work the one chain only before the first stitch—from then on, just work sc in the next stitch. Working the chain gives you a little extra height to reach the next stitch. Most instructions do not tell you to do this, but you should always add it. Work the reverse stitches loosely until you become comfortable with the stitch.

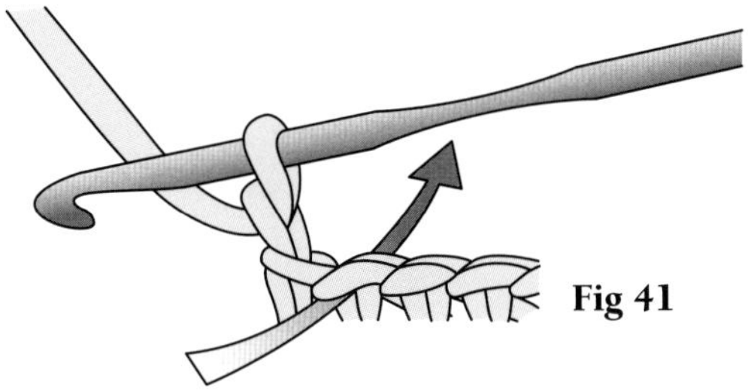

Fig 41

JOINING NEW YARN

You will often need to join a new ball of yarn, which should be done at the end of a row whenever possible. If you are running out of yarn, be sure you have enough yarn to complete the row before you start it. To join, work the last stitch of the row until one step of the stitch remains, then drop the yarn to the back, leaving the lp on the hook; leaving a 6" yarn end, hold the new yarn behind the work (**Fig 42**) and complete the last step of the stitch with the new yarn, make the turning chain with the new yarn, and continue with it. Cut off the old yarn, leaving a 6" end. Later weave in these two loose ends.

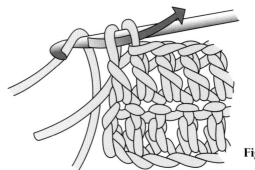

Fig 42

PART FOUR:
THE LANGUAGE OF CROCHET PATTERNS

Abbreviations

You have already learned the abbreviations for the basic crochet stitches: sl st, sc, hdc, dc and tr. Many other abbreviations are used in written patterns, and you need to learn them also.

Here are the standard abbreviations used in most patterns:

beg	beginning
bl	back loop
BP	back post
ch (s)	chain (s)
dc	double crochet
dec	decrease
fig	figure
fl(s)	front loop (s)
FP	front post
g	gram, grams
hdc	half double crochet
inc	increase
lp (s)	loop (s)
mm	millimeter
oz	ounce, ounces
patt	pattern
P	post
prev	previous
rem	remain or remaining
rep	repeat
rnd (s)	round (s)
sc	single crochet
sl	slip
sl st	slip stitch
st (s)	stitch, stitches
sp (s)	space (s)
sk	skip
tch	turning ch
tog	together
yd (s)	yard (s)
YO or yo	yarn over

Symbols

Several symbols are used to abbreviate and clarify patterns:

* The asterisk indicates a part of a pattern to be worked more than one time. The pattern might read "rep from * 3 times" or "rep from * three times more". So after working the specified instructions one time, work them as many more times as specified.

A double asterisk ** and a dagger † are used the same way as the single asterisk.

The number after a colon : or a double dash — at the end of a row or round indicates the number of stitches there should be at the end of the row or rnd.

Parentheses () or brackets [] enclose instructions that are to be worked the exact number of times immediately following them: (dc in next 2 sts, ch 2, skip 2 sts) 5 times. They can also be used to denote a group of stitches to be worked into the same space or stitch: (3 dc, ch 3, 3 dc) in next st.

PART FIVE:
TOOLS OF THE TRADE
All About Yarn

YARN WEIGHTS

Yarn is classified by **weight**, which really refers to its thickness. Yarns can be so very thin that they are used to make lace, or as fat as your little finger.

These are the yarn weights you will use most often:

Baby weight: A fine yarn that is used for baby clothes, and sometimes for socks.

Sport weight: Thicker than baby weight yarn; this is often used to make fashion garments or children's clothing

Double Knitting or DK weight: This yarn is just a bit thicker than sport weight, but usually can be substituted for sport yarn

Worsted weight: This is the weight used most often for afghans and other household items.

Bulky weight: A heavy yarn used mainly for craft or quick projects.

Tip: 4-ply yarn is a term often used mistakenly to refer to worsted weight yarn. All yarn is made up of a number of plies, or strands, that are twisted together to make the strand you will work with. Baby yarn can be made of four plies, and worsted yarn can be made of just two plies; it all depends on the thickness of each ply. So just because yarn is made of four plies does not mean it is worsted weight.

SPECIALTY YARNS

When you enter a yarn department, you may be overwhelmed by the wonderful variety of different yarn types and colors that are available to the crocheter. You'll find yarns that are fuzzy and fur-like, that have long "eyelashes" on them, that have metallic fibers twisted in, or that look like suede or velvet.

When you buy yarn, you need to buy the specific weight that is specified in the pattern you are planning to make, and you need to buy enough of it all at one time to complete the project. Yarns are dyed in batches, and unless the yarn says "no dye lot" you need to be sure each skein comes from the same dye lot because each lot may vary in color intensity. Yarns can also be discontinued suddenly and without warning, which could leave you with five rows to finish on your afghan, and no more yarn available.

You can, however, substitute one brand for another within the weight classification.

Crochet Hooks

You have been using a size H (5 mm) crochet hook for your practice lessons. This size, along with size G (4.5 mm), which is slightly smaller than the size H, and size I (5.5mm), which is slightly larger than the size H, are the three sizes most often used for working with worsted weight yarn.

Buying a crochet hook can be confusing, because of the way hooks are marked. Different manufacturers use different markings—some use a letter system, others use a numbering system. The most accurate way to choose a hook is go by the millimeter (mm) sizing, which refers to the hook's diameter. Here is a guide from the Craft Yarn Council:

CHOOSING THE HOOK SIZE

The pattern you are going to make will tell you the hook size that is suggested—but that is not written in stone! That just a starting point for testing your all-important gauge.

You'll need to work a gauge swatch (see page 22) to determine what size hook to use for any given project.

Crochet hooks are most often found made of aluminum or plastic, but you can also find them made of wood and other substances. There are also hooks made of steel, which are used for working with fine crochet thread, not with yarn.

Mm size	Letter size	Number size
2.25 mm	B	1
2.75 mm	C	2
3.25 mm	D	3
3.50 mm	E	4
3.75 mm	F	5
4.00 mm	G	6
4.50 mm	—	7
5.00 mm	H	8
5.50 mm	I	9
6.00 mm	J	10
6.50 mm	K	10 1/2
8.00 mm	L	11
9.00 mm	M or N	13
10.00 mm	N	15
12 mm	O	—
15.00 mm	P	—
16.00 mm	Q	—
19.00 mm	S	—

If you are using some older hooks, perhaps passed down by your mother or grandmother, they may not have the millimeter sizing.

PART SIX: DECORATIVE STITCH GALLERY

Using the basic stitches, you can create many decorative stitches that add interest to your work. Here are just a few of them you might like to try, then add the swatches to your samples.

Shell Stitch

There are many ways to make a shell stitch. Shells flare out on each side, so it is sometimes necessary to skip a stitch before and after the shell. Here is one type of shell.

Ch 10.

Row 1: Sc in the 2nd ch from hook and in each rem ch: 19 sc; ch 1, turn.

Row 2: Sc in each sc, ch 1, turn.

Row 3 (right side): Sc in the first sc, skip the next 2 sc; *in the next sc work a shell of (3 dc, ch 3, 3 dc); skip 2 sc, sc in the next sc; rep from *2 more times. Finish off; weave in ends.

Puff Stitch

This makes a soft "puff" on the right side of the work. When working puff stitches, be sure to pull the stitches up as high as the turning ch, and work them loosely but evenly.

Ch 20.

Row 1: Sc in the 2nd ch from hook and in each rem ch: 19 sc; ch 1, turn.

Row 2: Sc in each sc, ch 3 (counts as first dc of following row), turn.

Row 3 (right side): Dc in next sc, skip next sc; *YO, insert hook in next st and draw up a 1" lp; (YO, insert hook in same st and draw up a 1" lp) 4 times more: 11 lps now on hook; YO and draw through all 11 lps: you have made one Puff st; ch 1; skip the next sc, dc in next sc, skip next sc; repeat from * 2 more times, skip next sc, dc in last 2 stitches. Finish off; weave in ends.

Popcorn Stitch

These add a nice dimensional look to your work. Popcorns can be worked with 4 or 5 dc stitches; the more dc stitches, the more the popcorn will stick out.

Ch 20.

Row 1: Sc in the 2nd ch from hook and in each rem ch: 19 sc; ch 1, turn.

Row 2: Sc in each sc, ch 3 (counts as first dc of following row), turn.

Row 3 (right side): Dc in next sc, *skip next sc; work 4 dc in the next sc; draw the lp on the hook up slightly and remove the hook; insert the hook from front to back under both lps of the first dc of the 4-dc group, hook the dropped lp and draw it through, ch 1: one Popcorn stitch made; skip next sc, dc in next sc; rep from * across. Finish off; weave in ends.

Crossed Stitch

This is an easy stitch that is often used as a main fabric stitch. It is sometimes called Cross Stitch.

Ch 19.

Row 1: Sc in the 2nd ch from hook and in each rem ch: 18 sc; ch 1, turn.

Row 2: Sc in each sc, ch 3 (counts as first dc of following row), turn.

Row 3 (right side): *Skip the next sc, dc in next sc; working in front of dc just made, dc in the skipped sc: one Crossed stitch made; rep from * across the row to last st, dc in the last st. Finish off; weave in ends.

PART SEVEN: I'M GLAD YOU ASKED...

I'm sure you still have lots of questions about crochet. Here are the answers to some questions I've often been asked.

QUESTION: *My afghan pattern calls for a chain of 240 stitches. How in the world do I keep track of so many to be sure I have the right number?*

ANSWER: That's easy! Just place a small safety pin in every 20th stitch. When I have to make a chain that's really long, I do that. Then I place a safety pin in the last stitch and chain about 10 extra stitches. When you work the first row, you might sometimes accidentally skip a chain or two, and if so, you can use these extras at the end. If you don't need them, just pick out the beginning slip knot and unravel them.

QUESTION: *Working the first row into a starting chain is sometimes difficult. I've heard there is a way to work the chain and the first row at the same time. How do I do that?*

ANSWER: Here's how to work a starting chain and an sc row at the same time.

Step 1: Make a sl knot on hook and ch 2.

Step 2: Insert hook under top lp of 2nd ch from hook, YO and draw up a lp; YO and draw through both lps on hook.

Step 3: Insert hook under back lp of stitch just made, YO and draw up a lp; YO and draw through both lps on hook: 1 stitch made.

Repeat Steps 2 and 3 for as many stitches as you need. And there you have the starting chain and the first row of sc!

QUESTION: *I always check my gauge, but often I can get the exact stitch gauge, but not the row gauge. What do I do then?*

ANSWER: It's easy to adjust your row gauge. You will find the instructions for doing this under "To Adjust the Row Gauge" on page 21.

This first lp drawn up for any stitch is what I call the "magic lp", as it determines the height of your rows. Adjusting the height of this first lp works for sc, hdc, tr or any stitch.

QUESTION: *My Aunt says I should use 4-ply yarn for my first afghan, but at the store I couldn't find any yarn that said 4-ply. What do I do?*

ANSWER: What your Aunt probably meant was for you to use a weight of yarn called worsted weight. This yarn used to be called 4-ply, but not any more. Here's why.

Every yarn is made up of plies. A ply is one thin strand of fiber that is twisted with other strands to make a certain weight of yarn. This is fully explained on page 28 under Yarn Weights.

On the yarn label and often in patterns, you will see symbols identifying the weight of the yarn. These symbols, developed by the Craft Yarn Council, let you quickly identify the weight of the yarn you are looking at, or the weight of the yarn called for in the pattern. Here are these symbols and what they mean:

Symbol & Category Names	1 SUPER FINE	2 FINE	3 LIGHT	4 MEDIUM	5 BULKY	6 SUPER BULKY
Type of Yarns in Category	Sock, Fingering, Baby	Sport, Baby	DK, Light Worsted	Worsted, Afghan, Aran	Chunky, Craft, Rug	Bulky, Roving

QUESTION: *If I substitute the same weight of one yarn brand for the same weight of another, can I be sure it will give me the same results?*

ANSWER: Not always. Within the weight standards, there are variations. In worsted weight there can be light, medium and heavy worsted weights. So it's important that you check your gauge. With the light weights, you may need a larger hook to get the gauge, or a smaller hook to get the gauge with a heavy worsted weight. The gauge swatch really is your best friend!

QUESTION: *I always buy the amount of yarn the pattern says, but lots of times I run out before the project is finished. Why does this happen?*

ANSWER: It could be several reasons. For example, you may have substituted a variegated yarn when a solid color was specified. You may not have noticed that the variegated yarns usually have fewer oz or yds per skein than the solid colors. You need to substitute by total oz or yds, not by number of skeins.

Or it could be that when you substituted brands of yarn, you chose a yarn that had fewer yds or oz per skein than the original one specified. If you are able to use the internet, you can visit the web sites of most yarn manufacturers, where you will usually find information on the yds or oz in each skein.

But the most likely reason is—you did not check your gauge! If your gauge is too big, chances are you will run out of yarn. If it's too small, you may wind up with an extra skein and a skimpy project!

QUESTION: *I don't want to crochet garments for myself any more because they never fit! Why don't they design patterns that fit?*

ANSWER: Your problem probably goes back once again to that nasty word "gauge". Look at this example. You've chosen a sweater pattern that looks like it would fit you. Your bust measures 34" and the finished garment size is given as 36". Looks good, but you just don't

have time or interest in making that 4" gauge swatch, so you plunge right in. When you try on the finished garment—yikes! It's too big!

Here's what probably happened.

The gauge for the garment is given as 14 sts = 4".

Now you check the gauge on your finished garment: you find it has 13 sts = 4". Well, that's only one stitch off the gauge, so it can't hurt, can it? Let's see.

It's one st off in every 4"; the finished sweater is supposed to be 36". Divided by 4 that's 9. So the whole sweater will be 9 sts too big; at 13 sts = 4" that's a grand total of about 2¾" too large. So—that extra one stitch your gauge was off made a big difference.

QUESTION: *I ran out of yarn for an afghan I'm making, so I went back to the store and bought more. When I worked a few rows with it, I realized it didn't really match the first one. Why was the color so different? The new skein had the same color name as the others.*

ANSWER: You've now found out about dye lots! Yarn is dyed in batches, and the colors can differ from dye lot to dye lot. So you need to look at the yarn label and find where it gives you the number of the dye lot for that particular skein. Be sure you buy all the same dye lot for a project. Chances are when you go back another day, you may not be able to match the dye lot.

There are some yarns that are labeled "no dye lot". Usually, these will match whenever you buy them, but not always. To be safe, when I'm making a big project I always buy at least one more skein that the pattern says is needed. You can always use up these skeins for small items later.

QUESTION: *I'm making a bulky item, and it says to work with 2 strands of yarn held together. Wouldn't it be better to wind the two strands into one ball and work from that?*

ANSWER: No! Never do that! If you do, you'll find that as you work the strands won't pull along evenly, and pretty soon you'll have a big mess on your hands. Always work from two separate balls or skeins, or from opposite ends of a pull skein.

QUESTION: *At the start of my pattern it says, "Multiple of 4 plus 2 chains." I have no idea what that means. What do I do?*

ANSWER: Unless you are going to change the number of stitches in the pattern, you don't have to do anything, that is just there for information. A multiple is the number of stitches needed to work a given pattern stitch. Multiples are helpful to designers and to you if you plan to make a project, say an afghan, wider or narrower than the pattern specifies.

A multiple of 4 plus 2 means that to work the stitch pattern, you need any number of chains divisible by 4 (such as 16. 32, 48, etc) plus an additional 2 chains.

If you want to make the afghan wider, you would need to add chains in multiples of 4; or to make it narrower, you would need to subtract chains in multiples of 4. The "plus 2" is added only once.

QUESTION: *I want to crochet a hat for my 10-year-old niece, but I don't know what size to make it. How do I know how big her head is?*

Here are the average head size circumferences and hat depth for both adults and children:

	Circumference	**Depth**
Baby	14" - 15"	5" - 6"
Toddler	16"	7"
Child to 12 years	18" - 19"	8 - 8½"
Adult female	20" to 22	9" to 10":
Adult male	22" to 23"	10½" - 11"

Depth will depend on the style of the hat; add additional depth for a turn-up brim. Most crochet work is fairly stretchy, so allow for that in planning the circumference.

QUESTION: *Sometimes on patterns—especially in magazines—I notice a horizontal bar divided into sections with some shaded and some not. What does that mean?*

ANSWER: That is the Craft Yarn Council's symbol to indicate the skill level of a pattern. When one section of the bar is shaded, it indicates a beginner pattern; four shaded sections indicate a pattern for experienced crocheters. Here is how they work:

1 **BEGINNER**		Projects for first-time crocheters using basic stitches. Minimal shaping.
2 **EASY**		Projects using yarn with basic stitches, repetitive stitch patterns, simple color changes and simple shaping and finishing.
3 **INTERMEDIATE**		Projects using a variety of techniques, such as basic lace patterns or color patterns, mid-level shaping and finishing.
4 **EXPERIENCED**		Projects with intricate stitch patterns, techniques and dimensions, such as non-repeating patterns, multi-color techniques, fine threads, small hooks, detailed shaping and refined finishing.

PART EIGHT:
EASY CROCHET PROJECTS

Now that you've learned all the basic techniques of crochet, here are some projects to try that are perfect for the beginning crocheter.

Hat and Scarf Set

Size

Hat: Fits 20" to 23" head
Scarf: 8" x 46"

Materials

Worsted weight yarn,
14 oz off white
Note: *Photographed model made with Red Heart®
Classic™ #0111 Eggshell*
Size N (9 mm or 10 mm) crochet hook (or size
   required for gauge)
Note: *Different hook manufacturers make their
   N hooks in different mm sizes; either size will
   work for this project.*
Size K (6.5 mm) crochet hook
Yarn needle

Hat Gauge

First 2 rnds of hat = 2¼" with N hook and 2
   strands of yarn held tog

Scarf Gauge

3 (sc, ch 3) groups = 3¼" with N hook and 2
   strands of yarn held tog

Hat Instructions

Starting at top with larger hook and 2 strands of
yarn held tog, ch 4; join with a sl st in first ch
made to form a ring.

Rnd 1 (right side): Ch 3 (counts as a dc on this
and following rnds), work 11 dc in ring; join
with a sl st in 3rd (top) ch of beg ch-3. Counting
beg ch-3 as a stitch, you now have 12 dc.

Rnd 2: Ch 3, dc in same ch as joining (this is an
increase); 2 dc in each rem dc; join with sl st as
before in beg ch-3: 24 dc.

Rnd 3: Ch 3, 2 dc in next dc; *dc in next dc, 2
dc in next dc; rep from * around, join as before:
36 dc.

Rnd 4: Ch 1, sc in same ch as joining; *ch 3,
skip next dc, sc in next dc; rep from * 16 times
more, ch 3, join with a sl st in beg sc: 18 ch-3
sps.

Rnd 5: Sl st in next ch-3 sp, ch 1, sc in same sp;
*ch 3, sc in next ch-3 sp; rep from * 16 times
more, ch 3, join with a sl st in beg sc.

Rnds 6 through 13: Rep Rnd 5.

At end of Rnd 13, change to smaller size hook
and work rolled brim. Changing to the smaller
hook creates the roll effect.

BRIM

Rnd 14: Ch 2 (counts as hdc on this and following rnds); *2 hdc in next ch-3 sp, hdc in next sc;
rep from * 16 times more; 2 hdc in next ch-3 sp,
join with a sl st in 2nd ch of beg ch-2: 54 hdc.

Rnd 15: Ch 2; * 2 hdc in next hdc, hdc in next
hdc; rep from * 25 times more, join as before: 81
hdc.

Rnd 16: Ch 2, hdc in each hdc around, join as
before.

Rnds 17 and 18: Rep Rnd 16.

Rnd 19: Ch 1, sc in each st around; join. Finish
off; weave in all ends. Roll up brim.

Scarf Instructions

With smaller hook and 2 strands of yarn held
tog, ch 26.

Row 1: Sc in 2nd ch from hook and in each rem
ch; ch 1, turn: 25 sc.

Rows 2 and 3: Sc in each sc across, ch 1, turn.

Row 4: Change to larger hook; hdc in first sc;
*ch 3, skip 3 sc, hdc in next sc; rep from *
across, ch 1, turn: 6 ch-3 sps.

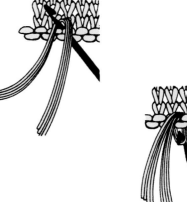

FRINGE

Cut yarn into strands each 24" long. Using 2 strands, folded in half, in each knot, draw the folded ends through every stitch in the bottom edge of each border.

Pull the loose ends through the folded section and draw the knot up firmly.

Note: Ch 1 does not count as hdc in this pattern.

Row 5: Hdc in first hdc, ch 3; *hdc in next ch-3 sp, ch 3; rep from * across, hdc in last hdc ch 1, turn: 6 ch-3 sps.

Rep Row 5 until scarf measures about 45" from beg ch; at end of last row, ch 1, turn.

BORDER

Row 1: Change to smaller hook; sc in first hdc, 3 sc in next ch-3 sp; * sc in next hdc, 3 sc in next ch-3 sp; rep from * across: 25 sc; ch 1, turn.

Row 2: Sc in each sc across, ch 1, turn.

Rows 3: Sc in each sc across. Finish off; weave in ends.

Trim fringe evenly.

Baby Afghan and Bonnet

Size

Afghan: 36" x 36"
Bonnet: Fits up to 18" head

Materials

Worsted weight yarn,
  10½ oz off white
  6 oz green
  3½ oz rose
  3 oz yellow
*Note: Photographed model made with Bernat®
  Berella "4"® #08949 Natural, #01235 Soft
  Green, #08814 Pale Antique Rose and Red
  Heart® Classic™ #0261 Maize*
Yarn needle
Size H (5 mm) crochet hook (or size required
  for afghan gauge)
Size G (4 mm) crochet hook (or size required
  for bonnet gauge)

Gauge

For afghan, one square with H hook = 7"
For bonnet, one square with G hook = 5"

Stitch Guide

Cluster (Cl): (YO insert hook in specified ring
or sp and draw up a lp, YO and draw through 2
lps on hook) 3 times; YO and draw through rem
4 lps on hook: Cl made.

Beg Cluster (beg Cl): Ch 3; (YO, insert hook in
ring or sp and draw up a lp, YO and draw
through 2 lps on hook) twice; YO and draw
through rem 3 lps on hook: beg Cl made.

Petal: (Cl ch 3, Cl) in same sp.

Afghan Instructions

SQUARE (make 25)

With yellow and larger hook, ch 6; sl st in first
ch to form a ring.

Rnd 1: Ch 3, (YO, insert hook in ring and draw
up a lp, YO and draw through 2 lps on hook)

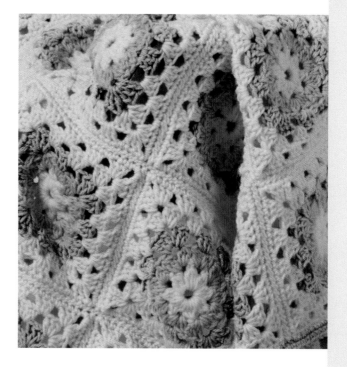

twice; YO and draw through rem 3 lps on hook:
beg Cl made; ch 3, (Cl in ring, ch 3) 7 times; sl st
in top ch of beg ch-3 to join; counting beg Cl,
you have made 8 Cl sts. Finish off yellow.

Rnd 2: Join rose with a sl st in any ch-3 sp; in
same sp work (beg Cl, ch 3, Cl): petal made; *in
next ch-3 sp work (Cl, ch 3, Cl): petal made; rep
from * 6 times more, sl st in top of beg Cl to
join; you have made 8 petals; finish off rose.

Rnd 3: Join green with a sl st in any ch-3 sp of
Rnd 2; ch 3 (this ch counts as the first dc of the
rnd); in same sp work (2 dc, ch 3, 3 dc): first
corner made; ch 1, 3 dc in ch-3 sp of next petal
(this makes the first side of the square), ch 1;
*in next ch-3 sp work (3 dc, ch 3, 3 dc): corner
made; ch 1, 3 dc in next ch-3 sp for side, ch 1;
rep from * twice more, sl st in 3rd ch of beg
ch-3. Finish off green.

Rnd 4: Join off white with a sl st in any corner
ch-3 sp; ch 3, (2 dc, ch 3, 3 dc) in same sp; ch 1,
(3 dc in next ch-1 sp, ch 1) twice; * in next corner ch-3 sp work (3 dc, ch 3, 3 dc) for corner;
ch 1, (3 dc in next ch-1 sp, ch 1) twice; rep from
* twice more, sl st in top ch of beg ch-3.

Rnd 5: Sl st in next 2 dc and into ch-3 corner sp; (ch 3, 2 dc, ch 3, 3 dc) in same sp for corner; ch 1, (3 dc in next ch-1 sp, ch 1) 3 times, work corner; rep from * twice more, (3 dc in next ch-1 sp, ch 1) 3 times, sl st in top ch of beg ch-3.

Rnd 6: Ch 1, sc in same ch as sl st, sc in next 2 dc, 3 sc in next ch-3 sp for corner; sc in each dc and in each ch-1 sp around, working 3 sc in each rem ch-3 corner sp; at end, join with sl st in beg sc. Finish off; weave in all yarn ends.

ASSEMBLY

Join squares in 5 rows of 5 squares each.

To join, hold two squares with right sides together. Carefully matching sts, sew together along one side with overcast st (see page 23) starting in one center corner st and ending in opposite corner center st. Join additional squares in same manner until you have 5 squares joined in a strip. Join 4 more strips in same manner. Hold two strips with right sides tog and starting in right corner, sew strips tog in same manner, again matching sts and corners. Continue until all strips are joined.

BORDER

Rnd 1: Hold afghan with right side facing you. Join green with a sl st in upper right-hand corner in center corner st; ch 1, 3 sc in same st; sc across afghan top, working 1 sc in each st of each square and one sc in each joining, to next corner; in corner work 3 sc; continue in this manner around, join with sl st in beg sc. Finish off green.

Rnd 2: Hold afghan with right side facing you; join rose with a sl st in center corner st at upper right, 3 sc in same st; sc in each sc around afghan, working 3 sc in each rem corner st, adjusting sts as needed to keep work flat. Finish off rose; weave in all ends.

Bonnet Instructions

SQUARE (make 4)

With smaller hook, work Rnds 1 through 3 of Afghan Square instructions.

Rnd 4: Join off white in any ch-3 corner sp; ch 1, 3 sc in same sp; sc in each dc and each sp around, sl st in beg sc to join. Finish off; weave in ends.

Join in strip of 3 in same manner as afghan joining; sew 4th square to center square, fold in sides to form a cup (**Fig 1**) and sew with overcast st.

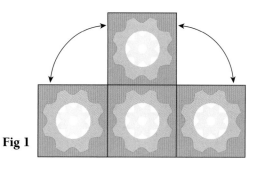

Fig 1

BORDER, BRIM AND TIES

Hold bonnet with right side facing you and row of 3 squares at top. With smaller hook, join off white with a sl st in center sc of 3-sc group at corner of square at your right.

For first tie, ch 48, sl st in 2nd ch from hook and in each rem ch; join with sl st in beg sl st.

For ruffled brim, sl st in next sc to left; ch 3, dc in same st; *3 dc in next sc, 2 dc in next sc; rep from * across the 3 squares, sl st into center sc of 3-sc group at corner of square at your left.

For second tie, ch 48, sl st in 2nd ch from hook and in each rem ch; join with sl st in beg sl st.

For back and sides border, turn bonnet so that right side is still facing and opposite edge is at top; *sc in next sc; draw up a lp in each of next 2 sc, YO and draw through all 3 lps on hook: decrease made; rep from * across to First tie, join with sl st. Finish off; weave in ends.

Granny Ripple Afghan

Size

36" x 50"

This afghan combines two favorite crochet themes: the ripple and the granny. Together they create a beautiful afghan that you can make in your favorite three colors.

Materials

Worsted weight yarn,
  12 oz white
  8 oz rose
  8 oz green

Note: *Photographed model made with Red Heart® Super Saver® #313 Aran, # 374 Country Rose, and # 631 Light Sage.*

Size H (5 mm) crochet hook (or size required for gauge)

Gauge

14 dc = 4"
7dc rows = 4"

To check your gauge, make the following gauge swatch. When finished it should measure 4" square. If it is too large, make another gauge swatch with a smaller hook; if it is too small, make another gauge swatch with a larger hook. Do not begin the afghan until you have the correct gauge. If you have the correct stitch gauge, but not the row gauge, see "To Adjust the Row Gauge" on page 22.

Gauge Swatch

With white, ch 15.

Row 1: Sc in 2nd ch from hook and in each rem ch: 14 sc; ch 3 (this counts as the first dc of the following row), turn.

Row 2: Dc in next sc and in each rem dc; ch 3, turn.

Rows 3 through 8: Rep Row 2. At end of last row, finish off.

Place swatch on a flat surface; without stretching, carefully measure. It should be 4" wide x 4" long, counting the dc rows but not the beg sc row.

Stitch Guide

A cluster stitch is used in this afghan; it is abbreviated Cl. Here is how to make it.

CLUSTER:

Step 1: YO, insert hook in specified st and draw up a lp to height of a dc: 3 lps now on hook.

Step 2: YO and draw through first 2 lps on hook: 2 lps remain on hook.

Step 3: YO again, insert hook into same st and draw up a lp to height of a dc: 4 lps now on hook.

Step 4: YO and draw through first 2 lps on hook: 3 lps remain on hook.

Step 5: YO and draw through all 3 lps: Cl made.

Note: *When making the YO sts, remember to bring yarn from back to front over the hook.*

Shell: Work (3 dc, ch 3, 3 dc) all in the specified st or sp.

Instructions:

With white, ch 163.

Row 1: Sc in 2nd ch from hook and in each rem ch: 162 sc; ch 3 (counts as first dc of next row), turn.

Row 2: Skip first 3 sc, (3 dc in next sc, skip next 2 sc) 3 times; in next sc work shell of (3 dc, ch 3, 3 dc); *(skip next 2 sc, 3 dc in next sc) twice, skip 2 sc; Cl in next sc, skip 4 sc, Cl in next sc; (skip 2 sc, 3 dc in next sc) twice; skip 2 sc, in next sc work shell of (3 dc, ch 3, 3 dc); rep from * to last 12 sc, skip 2 sc, (3 dc in next sc, sk 2 sc) 3 times, dc in last sc; ch 2, turn.

Note: *To work in space (sp) on following rows, work between Cls or 3-dc groups.*

Row 3: Skip first sp (between turning ch and next 3-dc group); 3 dc in each of next 3 sps; in next ch-3 sp work shell; *3 dc in each of next 2 sps, Cl in next sp, skip sp between Cls, Cl in next sp; 3 dc in each of next 2 sps, in next ch-3 sp work shell; rep from * across to last 4 sps; 3 dc in each of next 3 sps, dc in last sp (between last 3-dc group and turning ch-2); ch 2, turn.

Rep Row 3 once more with white, changing to new color in last dc; work turning ch-2 in new color.

Note: *See Joining New Yarn on page 25.*

Rep Row 3 for pattern, working in this color sequence:

3 rows green

3 rows rose

3 rows white

Work until piece measures about 48" long, ending with 3 white rows. Finish off; weave in ends.

Tank Top

Designed by Laura Gebhardt

You'll want to make this versatile and easy-to-make tank top in several colors. Try it in a multi-color yarn or a solid color, or even a textured yarn, which we used for our photographed model. The garment is made entirely in single crochet.

Sizes	Small	Medium	Large
Body Bust Measurements	32" - 34"	36" - 38"	40" - 42"
Finished Bust Measurements	34"	39"	44"

Materials

Worsted weight yarn,
  9 oz (for size small)
  10 oz (for size medium)
  11 oz (for size large)
Size I (5.5 mm) crochet hook (or size
  required for gauge)

Gauge

13 sc = 4"
15 sc rows = 4"

Note: Be sure to test your gauge before you start. Change hook size if necessary to achieve the specified gauge. Both stitch and row gauge are important to the correct fit of this garment. If you can get the stitch gauge, but not the row gauge, see "To Adjust the Row Gauge" on page 22.

Stitch Guide

Sc decrease (sc dec): (Insert hook in next st and draw up a lp) twice, YO and draw through all 3 lps on hook: sc dec made.

Note: To make the instructions easier to follow for a beginner, we have given them separately for each size.

Instructions for Size Small

BACK

Starting at bottom, ch 57.

Row 1: Sc in 2nd ch from hook and in each ch across: 56 sc; ch 1, turn.

Row 2: Sc in each sc; ch 1, turn.

Rows 3 through 10: Rep Row 2.

Row 11: Sc dec over first 2 sc, sc to last 2 sc, work sc dec: 54 sc; ch 1, turn.

Row 12: Rep Row 2.

Rows 13 and 14: Rep Rows 11 and 12: 52 sc.

Rows 15 and 16: Rep Row 2.

Row 17: 2 sc in first sc (increase made), sc across to last sc, 2 sc in last sc (increase made): 54 sc; ch 1, turn.

Row 18: Rep Row 2.

Row 19: Rep Row 17: 56 sc.

Rep Row 2 until piece measures 10" from beg chain; at end of last row, do not ch 1. Now you will begin to shape the armholes.

ARMHOLE SHAPING

Row 1 (right side): Sl st in first 4 sc, ch 1, sc in same st as last sl st and in each sc across to last 3 sts: 50 sc; ch 1, turn, leaving last 3 sts unworked. You now have 3 sts on each side which form the underarms.

Row 2: Sc dec over the first 2 sc, sc to last 2 sts, work sc dec: 48 sc; ch 1, turn.

Rows 3 through 7: Rep Row 2; at end of Row 7: 38 sc.

Row 8: Sc across; ch 1, turn.

Row 9: Rep Row 2: 36 sc.

Rows 10 through 15: Rep Rows 8 and 9 in sequence; at end of Row 15: 30 sc.

Rows 16 through 18: Rep Row 8.

Row 19: Rep Row 2: 28 sc.

Rows 20 through 22: Rep Row 8.

Row 23: Rep Row 2: 26 sc.

Row 24: Rep Row 8.

RIGHT SHOULDER SHAPING

Row 1 (right side): Sc in first 8 sc, ch 1, turn, leaving rem 18 sts unworked (the unworked sts will later be used for the neck and left shoulder).

Row 2: Sc dec over first 2 sts, sc across: 7 sc; ch 1, turn.

Row 3: Sc to last 2 sts, work sc dec: 6 sc; ch 1, turn.

Row 4: Sc dec over first 2 sts, sc across: 5 sc. Finish off; weave in yarn ends.

NECK AND LEFT SHOULDER SHAPING

Row 1: With right side facing, skip next 10 unworked sc on last row of armhole shaping (these sts form the bottom of the neckline); join yarn with sl st in next (11th) sc, ch 1, sc in same st as joining; sc in next 7 sc for left shoulder: 8 sc; ch 1, turn.

Row 2: Sc across to last 2 sc, work sc dec: 7 sc; ch 1, turn.

Row 3: Sc dec over first 2 sc, sc across: 6 sc; ch 1, turn.

Row 4: Rep Row 2: 5 sc. Finish off; weave in yarn ends.

FRONT

Work same as back to Armhole Shaping.

FRONT ARMHOLE SHAPING

Row 1 (right side): Sl st in first 4 sc for under-arm, ch 1, sc in same st as last sl st and in each sc across to last 3 sts, ch 1 turn, leaving last 3 sts unworked for underarm: 50 sc.

Row 2: Sc dec over first 2 sts, sc to last 2 sts, work sc dec, ch 1, turn: 48 sc.

LEFT NECK AND ARMHOLE

Now you will divide the piece and work the left armhole and left side of the V-neck separately. You will be decreasing for both the neck (at the inside edge) and the armhole (at the outside edge) at the same time.

Row 1: Sc dec over the first 2 sc, sc in next 20 sc, work sc dec: 22 sc; ch 1, turn, leaving rem 24 sts unworked for right neck and armhole.

Row 2: Sc across to last 2 sc, work sc dec: 21 sc; ch 1, turn.

Row 3: Sc dec over first 2 sc, sc to last 2 sc, work sc dec: 19 sc; ch 1, turn.

Rows 4 and 5: Rep Rows 2 and 3. At end of Row 5: 16 sc.

Row 6: Sc across; ch 1, turn.

Row 7: Sc dec over first 2 sc, sc to last 2 sts, work sc dec: 14 sc; ch 1, turn.

Rows 8 through 13: Rep Rows 6 and 7 three times more in sequence: 8 sc.

Row 14: Rep Row 6.

Row 15: Rep Row 2: 7 sc.

Rows 16 and 17: Rep Rows 6 and 7: 5 sc.

Rows 18 through 25: Rep Row 6.

Row 26: Sc in each sc across. Finish off; weave in yarn ends.

RIGHT NECK AND ARMHOLE

Row 1: With right side facing, join yarn with sl st at center front in next unworked stitch; ch 1, sc dec over same st and next st; sc to last 2 sts, work sc dec: 22 sc; ch 1, turn.

Row 2: Sc dec over first 2 sc, sc across: 21 sc; ch 1, turn.

Row 3: Sc dec over first 2 sc, sc to last 2 sc, work sc dec: 19 sc; ch 1, turn.

Rows 4 and 5: Rep Rows 2 and 3. At end of Row 5: 16 sc.

Row 6: Sc across, ch 1, turn.

Row 7: Sc dec over first 2 sc, sc to last 2 sc, work sc dec: 14 sc; ch 1, turn.

Rows 8 through 13: Rep Rows 6 and 7 three times more in sequence: 8 sc.

Row 14: Rep Row 6.

Row 15: Rep Row 2: 7 sc; ch 1, turn.

Rows 16 and 17: Rep Rows 6 and 7: 5 sc.

Rows 18 through 25: Rep Row 6.

Row 26: Sc in each sc across. Finish off; weave in yarn ends.

FINISHING (FOR ALL SIZES)

Assembly

Hold front and back with right sides tog. Using overcast st (see page 23) and carefully matching rows and sts, sew shoulder and side seams. Turn piece right side out.

Neckline Edging

With right side facing, join yarn with sc in either shoulder seam on neck edge. Sc evenly around entire neck edge, adjusting sts as needed to keep work flat; join with sl st in beg sc. Finish off, weave in ends.

Armhole Edgings

With right side facing, join yarn with sc in one underarm seam. Sc evenly around entire armhole opening, adjusting sts as needed to keep work flat; join with sl st in beg sc. Finish off, weave in ends. Rep on opposite armhole.

Instructions for Size Medium

BACK

Starting at bottom, ch 65.

Row 1: Sc in 2nd ch from hook and in each ch across: 64 sc; ch 1, turn.

Row 2: Sc in each sc across, ch 1, turn.

Rows 3 through 10: Rep Row 2.

Row 11: Sc dec over first 2 sc, sc across to last 2 sc, work sc dec: 62 sc; ch 1, turn.

Row 12: Rep Row 2.

Rows 13 and 14: Rep Rows 11 and 12: 60 sc.

Rows 15 and 16: Rep Row 2.

Row 17: 2 sc in first sc (increase made), sc across to last sc, 2 sc in last sc (increase made): 62 sc; ch 1, turn.

Row 18: Rep Row 2.

Row 19: Rep Row 17: 64 sc.

Rep Row 2 until piece measures 10½" from beg chain; at end of last row, do not ch 1. Now you will begin to shape the armholes.

ARMHOLE SHAPING

Row 1 (right side): Sl st in first 5 sc, ch 1, sc in same st as last st st and in each sc across to last 4 sts: 56 sc; ch 1, turn, leaving last 4 sts unworked. You now have 4 sts on each side which form the underarms.

Row 2: Sc dec over the first 2 sc, sc to last 2 sc, work sc dec: 54 sc; ch 1, turn.

Rows 3 through 7: Rep Row 2; at end of Row 7: 44 sc.

Row 8: Sc across, ch 1, turn.

Row 9: Rep Row 2: 42 sc.

Rows 10 through 15: Rep Rows 8 and 9 in sequence; at end of Row 15: 36 sc.

Rows 16 through 18: Rep Row 8.

Row 19: Rep Row 2: 34 sc.

Rows 20 through 23: Rep Rows 16 through 19: 32 sc.

Rows 24 through 26: Rep Row 8.

RIGHT SHOULDER SHAPING

Row 1 (right side): Sc in first 10 sc, ch 1, turn, leaving rem 22 sts unworked (the unworked sts will later be used for the neck and left shoulder).

Row 2: Sc dec over first 2 sts, sc across: 9 sc; ch 1, turn.

Row 3: Sc across to last 2 sts, work sc dec: 8 sc; ch 1, turn.

Row 4: Sc dec over first 2 sts, sc across: 7 sc.

Row 5: Rep Row 3: 6 sc. Finish off, weave in yarn ends.

NECK AND LEFT SHOULDER SHAPING

Row 1: With right side facing, skip next 12 unworked sc on last row of armhole shaping (these sts form the bottom of the neckline); join yarn with sl st in next (13th) sc, ch 1, sc in same st as joining; sc in next 9 sc for left shoulder: 10 sc; ch 1, turn.

Row 2: Sc across to last 2 sc, work sc dec: 9 sc; ch 1, turn.

Row 3: Sc dec over first 2 sc, sc across: 8 sc; ch 1, turn.

Row 4: Sc across to last 2 sc, work sc dec: 7 sc.

Row 5: Rep Row 3: 6 sc; at end, do not ch 1. Finish off; weave in yarn ends.

FRONT

Work same as back to Armhole Shaping

FRONT ARMHOLE SHAPING

Row 1 (right side): Sl st in first 5 sc for under-arm, ch 1, sc in same st as last sl st and in each

sc across to last 4 sts, ch 1, turn, leaving last 4 sts unworked for underarm: 56 sc.

Row 2: Sc dec over first 2 sts, sc to last 2 sts, work sc dec, ch 1, turn: 54 sc.

LEFT NECK AND ARMHOLE

Now you will divide the piece and work the left armhole and left side of the V-neck separately. You will be decreasing for both the neck (on the inside edge) and the armhole (at the outside edge) at the same time.

Row 1: Sc dec over the first 2 sc, sc in the next 23 sc, work sc dec: 25 sc; ch 1, turn, leaving rem 27 sts unworked for right neck and armhole.

Row 2: Sc across to last 2 sc, work sc dec: 24 sc; ch 1, turn.

Row 3: Sc dec over first 2 sc, sc across to last 2 sc, work sc dec: 22 sc; ch 2, turn.

Rows 4 and 5: Rep Rows 2 and 3. At end of Row 5: 19 sc.

Row 6: Sc across; ch 1, turn.

Row 7: Sc dec over first 2 sc, sc to last 2 sc, work sc dec: 17 sc; ch 1, turn.

Rows 8 through 13: Rep Rows 6 and 7 three times more in sequence: 11 sc.

Row 14: Rep Row 6.

Row 15: Rep Row 2: 10 sc.

Rows 16 and 17: Rep Rows 6 and 7: 8 sc.

Row 18 through 21: Rep Rows 6 and 2; at end of last row: 6 sc.

Rows 22 through Row 29: Rep Row 6. At end of Row 29, finish off; weave in yarn ends.

RIGHT NECK AND ARMHOLE

Row 1: With right side facing, join yarn with sl st at center front in next unworked st; ch 1, work sc dec over same st and next st; sc across to last 2 sts, work sc dec: 25 sc; ch 1, turn.

Row 2: Sc dec over first 2 sc, sc across: 24 sc; ch 1, turn.

Row 3: Sc dec over first 2 sc, sc to last 2 sc, work sc dec: 22 sc; ch 1, turn.

Rows 4 and 5: Rep Rows 2 and 3. At end of Row 5: 19 sc.

Row 6: Sc across, ch 1, turn.

Row 7: Sc dec over first 2 sc, sc across to last 2 sc, work sc dec: 17 sc; ch 1, turn.

Row 8 through 13: Rep Rows 6 and 7 three times more in sequence. At end of Row 13: 11 sc.

Row 14: Rep Row 6.

Row 15: Rep Row 2: 10 sc; ch 1, turn.

Rows 16 and 17: Rep Rows 6 and 7: 8 sc.

Rows 18 through 21: Rep Rows 6 and 2: at end of last row: 6 sc.

Rows 22 through 29: Rep Row 6. At end of Row 29, finish off; weave in yarn ends.

FINISHING

Follow Finishing instructions on page 48.

Instructions for Size Large

Starting at bottom, ch 73.

Row 1: Sc in 2nd ch from hook and in each ch across: 72 sc; ch 1, turn.

Row 2: Sc in each sc across, ch 1, turn.

Rows 3 through 12: Rep Row 2.

Row 13: Sc dec over first 2 sc, sc to last 2 sc, work sc dec: 70 sc; ch 1, turn.

Row 14: Rep Row 2.

Rows 15 and 16: Rep Rows 13 and 14: 68 sc.

Rows 17 and 18: Rep Row 2.

Row 19: 2 sc in first sc (increase made), sc across to last sc, 2 sc in last st (increase made): 70 sc; ch 1, turn.

Row 20: Rep Row 2.

Rows 21 and 22: Rep Rows 19 and 20: 72 sc.

Rep Row 2 until piece measures 11" from beg ch; at end of last row, do not ch 1. Now you will begin to shape the armholes.

ARMHOLE SHAPING

Row 1 (right side): Sl st in first 6 sc, ch 1, sc in same st as last sl st and in each sc across to last 5 sc: 62 sc; ch 1, turn, leaving last 5 sts unworked. You now have 5 sts on each side which form the underarms.

Row 2: Sc dec over the first 2 sc, sc to last 2 sc, work sc dec: 60 sc; ch 1, turn.

Rows 3 through 7: Rep Row 2; at end of Row 7: 50 sc.

Row 8: Sc across, ch 1, turn.

Row 9: Rep Row 2: 48 sc.

Rows 10 through 15: Rep Rows 8 and 9 in sequence; at end of Row 15: 42 sc.

Rows 16 through 18: Rep Row 8.

Row19: Rep Row 2: 40 sc.

Rows 20 through 23: Rep Rows 16 through 19: 38 sc.

Rows 24 through 28: Rep Row 8.

RIGHT SHOULDER SHAPING

Row 1 (right side): Sc in first 12 sc; ch 1, turn, leaving rem 26 sts unworked (the unworked sts will later be used for the neck and left shoulder).

Row 2: Sc dec over the first 2 sc, sc across: 11 sc; ch 1, turn.

Row 3: Sc across to last 2 sc, work sc dec: 10 sc; ch 1, turn.

Row 4: Sc dec over first 2 sc, sc across: 9 sc.

Row 5: Rep Row 3: 8 sc; do not ch 1. Finish off; weave in yarn ends.

NECK AND LEFT SHOULDER SHAPING

Row 1: With right side facing, skip next 14 unworked sc on last row of armhole shaping (these sts form the bottom of the neckline); join yarn with sl st in next (15th) sc, ch 1, sc in same st as joining; sc in next 11 sc for left shoulder: 12 sc; ch 1, turn.

Row 2: Sc across to last 2 sc, work sc dec: 11 sc; ch 1, turn.

Row 3: Sc dec over first 2 sc, sc across: 10 sc; ch 1, turn.

Row 4: Sc to last 2 sc, work sc dec: 9 sc.

Row 5: Rep Row 3: 8 sc; at end of row, do not ch 1. Finish off; weave in yarn ends.

FRONT

Work same as back to Armhole Shaping.

FRONT ARMHOLE SHAPING

Row 1 (right side): Sl st in first 6 sc for under-arm, ch 1, sc in same st as last sl st and in each sc across to last 5 sc, ch 1, turn, leaving last 5 sts unworked for underarm: 62 sc.

Row 2: Sc dec over first 2 sc, sc to last 2 sc, work sc dec, ch 1, turn: 60 sc.

LEFT NECK AND ARMHOLE

Now you will divide the piece and work the left shoulder and left side of the V-neck separately. You will be decreasing for both the neck (at the inside edge) and the armhole (at the outside edge) at the same time.

Row 1: Sc dec over first 2 sc, sc in next 26 sc to last 2 sc, work sc dec: 28 sc; ch 1, turn, leaving rem 30 sts unworked for right neck and armhole.

Row 2: Sc across to last 2 sc, sc dec over last 2 sc: 27 sc; ch 1, turn.

Row 3: Sc dec over first 2 sc, sc to last 2 sc, work sc dec: 25 sc; ch 1, turn.

Rows 4 and 5: Rep Rows 2 and 3; at end of Row 5: 22 sc.

Row 6: Sc across, ch 1, turn.

Row 7: Sc dec over first 2 sc, sc to last sc, work sc dec: 20 sc; ch 1, turn.

Rows 8 through 13: Rep Rows 6 and 7 three times in sequence: 14 sc.

Row 14: Rep Row 6.

Row 15: Rep Row 2: 13 sc.

Rows 16 and 17: Rep Rows 6 and 7: 11 sc.

Rows 18 through 23: Rep Rows 6 and 2 three times more; at end of last row: 8 sc.

Rows 24 through 31: Rep Row 6; at end of last row, do not ch 1. Finish off; weave in yarn ends.

RIGHT NECK AND ARMHOLE

Row 1: With right side facing, join yarn with sl st at center front in next unworked st; ch 1, sc dec over same st and next sc; sc across to last 2 sc, work sc dec: 28 sc; ch 1, turn.

Row 2: Sc dec over first 2 sts, sc across: 27 sc; ch 1, turn.

Row 3: Sc dec over first 2 sc, sc to last 2 sc, work sc dec: 25 sc,

Rows 4 and 5: Rep Rows 2 and 3. At end of row 5: 22 sc.

Row 6: Sc across, ch 1, turn.

Row 7: Sc dec over first 2 sc, sc to last 2 sc, work sc dec: 20 sc; ch 1, turn.

Rows 8 through 13: Rep Rows 6 and 7 three times more in sequence. At end of last row: 14 sc.

Row 14: Rep Row 6.

Row 15: Rep Row 2: 13 sc.

Rows 16 and 17: Rep Rows 6 and 7: 11 sc.

Rows 18 through 23: Rep Rows 6 and 2 three times more; at end of last row: 8 sc.

Rows 24 through 32: Rep Row 6. At end of last row, do not ch 1. Finish off; weave in yarn ends.

FINISHING

Follow Finishing Instructions on page 48.

Headband

This pretty band is crocheted working in the back loops only of each row, which creates a type of ribbing that stretches to fit most head sizes. It is worked with two strands of yarn held together.

Size

Fits up to 23" head

Materials

Worsted weight yarn,
  3 oz blue
Note: Photographed model made with Red Heart® Classic™ #0382 Country Blue
Size J (6 mm) crochet hook (or size required for gauge)
Yarn needle

Gauge

3 sc = 1" with 2 strands of yarn held tog

Stitch Guide

Sc decrease (sc dec): Draw up a lp in each of next 2 sts, YO and draw through all 3 lps on hook: sc dec made.

Note: If you are using yarn from one skein, wind half of it into a separate ball so that you can use 2 strands held together.

Instructions

With 2 strands of yarn held tog, ch 6.

Row 1 (right side): Sc in 2nd ch from hook and in each rem ch: 5 sc; ch 1, turn.

Note: From here on, throughout pattern work in back loop only of each st.

Rows 2 through 16: Sc in each sc, ch 1, turn.

Row 17: 2 sc in first sc (increase made), sc in each sc to last sc, 2 sc in last sc (increase made): 7 sc; ch 1, turn.

Rows 18 through 20: Sc in each sc, ch 1, turn.

Row 21: Rep Row 17: 9 sc.

Row 22: Sc in each sc, ch 1, turn.

Row 23: Rep Row 17: 11 sc.

Rows 24 through 31: Sc in each sc, ch 1, turn.

Row 32: Sc dec over first 2 sc; sc in each sc to last 2 sts, sc dec over last 2 sts: 9 sc; ch 1, turn.

Row 33: Sc in each sc, ch 1, turn.

Row 34: Rep Row 32: 7 sc.

Rows 35 through 38: Sc in each sc; ch 1, turn.

Row 39: Rep Row 32: 5 sc.

Rows 40 through 53: Sc in each sc, ch 1, turn.

Row 54: Sc in each sc; finish off leaving a 10" yarn end.

Thread yarn end into yarn needle; with right sides tog, carefully matching sts, sew Row 1 and Row 54 tog into a ring. Weave in remaining end.